Praise for

Hold My Thoughts Captive

"If you are looking for some practical and Godly answers on how to take your thought life back, you have picked up the right book. What a wonderful book written for such a time as this. Blessed!"

--Cathy Eldridge

"Praise God for this book and the author. We need to learn to "Hold our Thoughts Captive." This book gives us great things to think about.

Why change your thoughts? There is no change in life without mind change. Our ways, our actions, our emotions, sometimes our friends will change. Mind change brings positive thoughts, positive thought gives positive actions. Our thoughts are very important. Please read this book, it will help you and bless you."

--Pastor Alma

"Even as a Christian, I have struggled with feelings of inadequacy my entire life. I never really understood where those feelings came from and I certainly didn't know how to process them or how to dispel the lies that I believed about myself.

In this book and workbook, Terry teaches you how to identify your negative self-image and emotions and where they have come from. She then shows you how to apply the Word of God to those places to change your mindset and to help you start believing that what God says about you is the absolute truth.

This book has been a life changer for me!"

--Sherri DeSorcy

"Terry's book is well thought out and a great roadmap to realign our thoughts with God's word."

--Liv Brownell

"This book will reach millions. God is going to put it in the hands of millions to change their way of thinking. They will be able to truly think with love rather than anger or fear. God will show them how amazing they are through this book and their personal processing. God is so good. He will change the world with this book. Many people will find His love and peace.

Lord, please allow every reader to find peace through the words you had Terry write. Please allow them to start thinking in your way, through love. Allow them to have such positive thoughts that they affect those around them to also start thinking positively. Thank you so much for allowing this book to be. Your love will reach so many people because of it. In Jesus name Amen."

--Pond Treasures LLC

"Absolutely amazing! I love how it takes you layer by layer on identifying emotions and processing through them. I ABSOLUTELY LOVE THIS BOOK!!"

--Alexandria Mattfield

Hold My Thoughts Captive

Understanding Our Thoughts

Terry Pond LPCA

Hold My Thoughts Captive
By Terry Pond LPCA

All Scripture is taken from the Holy Bible, New International Version®, NIV® Copyright © 1973, 1978, 1984, 2011 by Biblica, Inc.® Used by permission. All rights reserved worldwide.
Paperback ISBN 978-1-960046-00-0
eBook ISBN 978-1-960046-02-4
Hardback ISBN 978-1-960046-01-7
Published in the United States by Pond Treasures LLC.
Printed in the United States of America.

Contents

Hold My Thoughts Captive

Introduction

Author's Note

It is encouraged to take notes throughout the book for a better understanding of God and self. With the paper back and hard back versions blank pages have been provided to allow you to cut, tear, rip, and leave in to take notes, write emotions, write thoughts, bible verses, draw, doodle, sketch, to rip, or tear apart. These pages in the back and the ones throughout the book are designed to help you work through your emotions and thoughts throughout the exercise and to be able to do the exercise more than once and within the book itself. Amazon Kindle should allow you to take notes throughout, or you can use a notebook, a piece of paper, a napkin; anything will do. Find what is right for you, your emotions, and your thoughts.

Soon you will understand your thoughts, through God's word. You will want to do this exercise more than once. It is recommended getting paper or buying a physical copy to allow you to do the exercise many times. This exercise will take you into a place where you can capture your thoughts and push them into God's interpretation, otherwise seen as a positive version of the thoughts.

This book might be small, but it is a life changer.

"We take captive every thought to make it obedient to Christ." (2 Corinthians 10:5, NIV)

"Above all else, guard your heart, for everything you do flows from it." (Proverbs 4:23, NIV)

Chapter One

Thinking with God

The Bible is clear; you need to hold your thoughts captive and align all thoughts with the Bible. In many cases we believe negative thoughts about ourselves that are not biblical and according to the word. If you believe the negative, you live the negative. Living in the negative can cause unhappiness, sadness, depression, anxiety, and other dysfunctions. In order to change this we need to start to understand where our thoughts come from. Then we can start to forgive and create new thoughts based on what Gods word says about us. "Forgive as the Lord forgave you," (Colossians 3:13, NIV).

As we strive to walk in the purpose God has for us, we first need to correct what is not Godly. Our sins are forgiven but our mind keeps tally of all the negative thoughts and puts them on repeat. When we start to take those thoughts captive, we can replace them with Godly thoughts. "For I know the plans I have for you," declares the LORD "plans to prosper you and not to harm you, plans to give you hope and a future," (Jeremiah 29:11, NIV). God has a purpose for all of us. When we align our thoughts with God, we free ourselves from the negative thoughts. The Lord replied, "My presence will go with you, and I will give you rest," (Exodus 33:14, NIV).

Notes

17

When we live in God's purpose, we find joy and peace in everything we do. You were born "for such a time as this," (Esther 4:14, NIV). Striving for peace allows our bodies to function in the way God has intended. "A heart at peace gives life to the body," (Proverbs 14:30, NIV). "Peace I leave with you; my peace I give you... Do not let your hearts be troubled," (John 14:27, NIV). Let's hold our thoughts captive to better understand Gods purpose for us and live in the joy and peace God has given us.

Throughout this book you will be asked to take inventory of your thoughts and emotions. This means check with you. See if you have additional emotions or thoughts that need to be acknowledged. This is just a section to acknowledge these emotions and thoughts. When we acknowledge them, it gives the opportunity to understand ourselves and find grace and love for ourselves.

Processing emotions can be very hard and looks and feels different for each person. When this book mentions; process the emotion, it means process them however is correct for you. If you don't know how to process them, follow the exercise within the next pages. Each section will have space to write your thoughts or emotions.

Notes

Think of something that feels angry. Write down what feels angry.

_____

_____

_____

Where do you feel this anger? Arms? Head? Legs?

_____

_____

_____

How does it feel? Fuzzy? Hot? Cold? Heavy?

_____

_____

_____

Now look back at what you wrote. Anger for me is tightness in my arms and shoulders. What/where is anger for you?

_____

_____

_____

Now that we know what angry is for us how do we process it? We need to express the anger. Depending on each individual it could be journaling about the emotion, or it could be making a growling noise and stating, "I am Mad!" Sometimes it looks different according to the level of the emotion. Maybe level 3 of anger is growling, and a level 7 is journaling. Level 10 could be breaking something.

Notes

21

The goal of processing emotions is to express it and let it out. If we hold the emotions in without expressing, they can come out in explosions, physical issues, or in ways we can't control. Throughout this book emotions will come up. There will be reminders to acknowledge your emotions and thoughts. It's important to acknowledge your emotions; this will help with understanding the full impact of the emotion(s) on your thought(s).

Write down the ways you express anger.

_____

_____

_____

Changing your thoughts can be very difficult and slow. In order to do that you must identify the thoughts you want to change first. When you think of the negative thoughts you have swirling around in your head, pull one of them out. What is the thought telling you? In some cases, there is an underlying core thought. These core thoughts are things such as "I am not good enough", "I am alone", or "I am not loved".

As you think of this core thought let's make it pliable. Write it down on a piece of paper. Hold the paper and look at the thought. Should it be a color? Should it be written differently? Should it be written in a different font? How would you change it?

Now think about what is a positive thought that would cancel out the negative thought, such as "I am not good enough" lets change that to "I am good enough".

Notes

Chapter Two

Identify a Negative Thought

When you sit alone, and your thoughts start what is the thought that stands out to you most? As you sort through the thoughts how are you feeling? During this example we will be taking an inventory of our thoughts and emotions. As you take this inventory pay attention to where you feel each emotion and the reaction you have. It is important to understand your emotions and thoughts in order to better understand who you are as a person.

What are some of the negative thoughts you identified in your head?

_____

_____

_____

For this book we are going to use the negative thought "I am not good enough" because it is a common negative thought. We are going to walk through the way to understand the process of taking each thought captive and changing it if we can.

Notes

You will first write the thought down. Write it in the middle of the paper giving room to write around the thought.

I AM NOT GOOD ENOUGH!

As you look at the example what do you see? I see it is all in caps and it is written as if someone might be angry. If it was a text message it would be yelling at us. As we read it yelling at us how do we feel about this example? If it was your own core thought, would it be written differently? Would it be in color? How would you change it to match your core thought of not feeling good enough?

I am not good enough is common because many people feel they just don't do things the correct way or they don't have the understanding or knowledge to do it the way that someone else wants it done.

As you think about being not good enough how do you feel?

Is there scripture that makes this statement "I am not good enough" true?

Notes

Chapter Three

Processing Your Emotions around Your Thoughts

As you look at the statement take inventory of how you feel. This is not only the emotion you feel but also in your body. Are your shoulders tight? Are you in any discomfort? Do you see each word with a different feeling? When you look at "I" how do you feel about you? Maybe you have no feelings about any of it. Perhaps you have become numb. The emotions, surrounding the statement, have become too much you have turned every emotion and feeling off when you think "I am not good enough".

As we hold our thoughts captive it will be important to start to understand the full impact of the thought. It's time to turn the feelings back on.

"Blessed is the one who perseveres under trial." (James 1:12, NIV)

As you look at the example you will see it is all in caps and very straight lined. Let's take inventory of how we feel. Read the statement "I am not good enough" out loud.

What emotions come up?

_____

_____

_____

Notes

29

For me; it's sadness, anger, frustration, and devastation.

Do you have any Discomfort in your body?

_____

_____

_____

      For me this statement is heavy. It sits on my shoulders and chest, and it is a lot of pressure. It is almost crushing, it's so heavy.
      Now let's look at the way it's written. It's all in capitals. If you and I were texting it would be yelling at us, and the exclamation marks says it may be screaming at us. Each word is almost all different in sizes. "I" is bigger than all the other words. "Am" is the smallest word. It seems as if the "am" is sinking into the thought. Almost like it is stuck in the heavy and crushing feeling of sadness, anger, frustration, and devastating emotion.

```
┌─────────────────────────────────────────────┐
│                                             │
│                                             │
│     I  AM  NUT GOOD  ENOUGH!                │
│                                             │
│                                             │
└─────────────────────────────────────────────┘
```

Notes

31

It's time to add emotions and feelings to our paper.

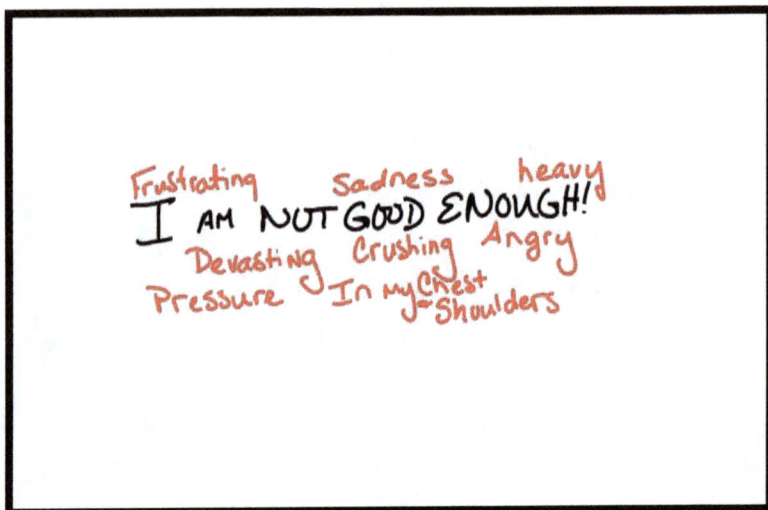

Frustrating   Sadness   heavy
I AM NOT GOOD ENOUGH!
Devasting Crushing Angry
Pressure In my Chest
              Shoulders

Now as we look at our paper, we see the thought that has caused frustration, sadness, anger, devastation, and a crushing heaviness. This thought has a lot of power over you. How do you feel knowing this thought has this much power?

_____

_____

_____

Notes

Chapter Four

History of Thoughts

As you think of the negative thought, think back to where you heard this thought and who may have said it. In some cases, the thoughts could have been created at an event. Perhaps at a sporting event and you needed to preform, and you felt you couldn't match that expectation. As you remember the event what was said and by whom was it said?

_____

_____

_____

Many People have heard THEY ARE NOT GOOD ENOUGH. This could have been heard from family members, teachers, friends, and as mentioned; events.

Notes

Let's start to include these people and events on our page.

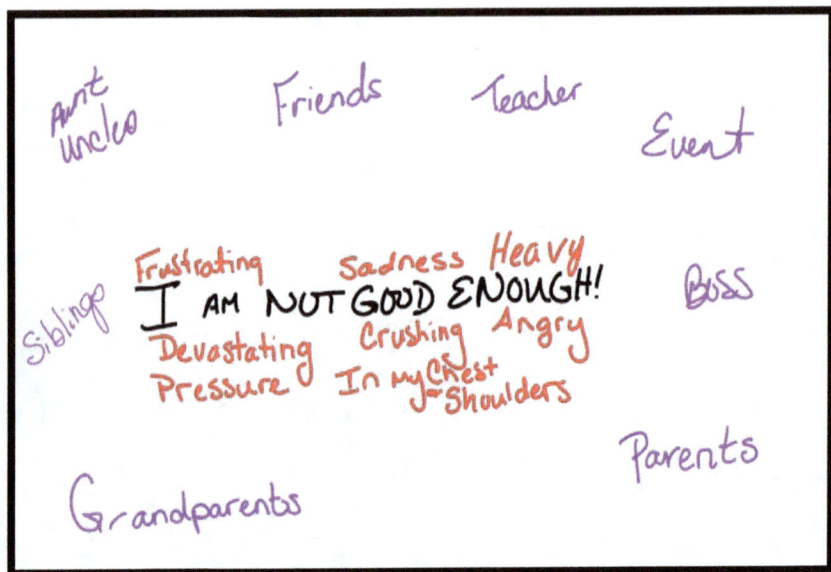

As you add people to your paper start to take inventory about how you feel with each person. Maybe you have a sadness when you think of one person, make a note of that. As you take inventory and add notes around each person, add any thoughts you may have as well.

_____

_____

_____

Notes

In some cases, forgiveness maybe needed. Perhaps it's time to forgive? Here is room to write them down and start the forgiveness process:

_____

_____

_____

Here is a suggestion for a prayer as you forgive them:

Dear God, thank you for today, tomorrow, and yesterday. Thank you for filling me with your love as I walk through the process of changing my thoughts. As I look at where my thoughts may have come from, I ask you to stand with me as I forgive those that may have contributed to these thoughts and emotions. I forgive everyone on the list above. I release the thoughts and emotions to you, God. I thank you for walking with me as I find peace and love. In Jesus name Amen.

You can write your own prayer here:

_____

_____

_____

Notes

As you look at the paper you may not have added someone that has reinforced the negative thought every day; you. You must add yourself to the paper.

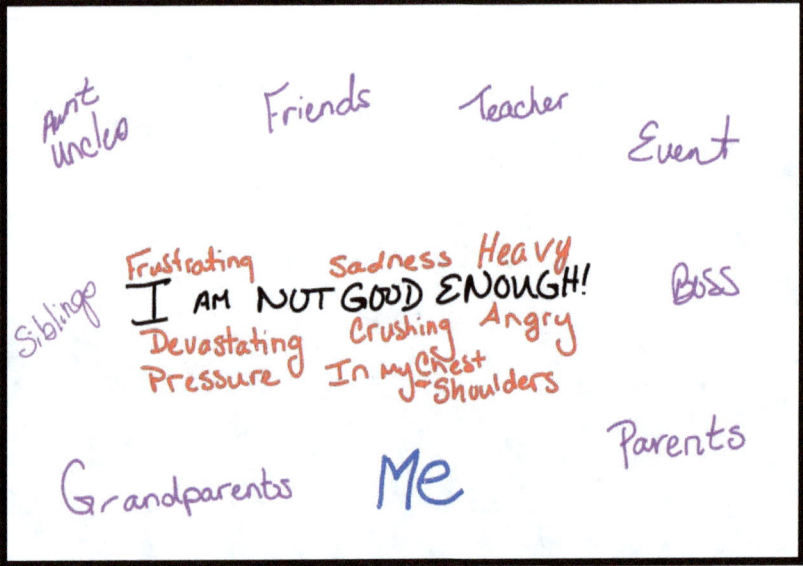

Aunt
Uncle   Friends   Teacher
                                              Event

Siblings   Frustrating   Sadness Heavy   Boss
           I AM NOT GOOD ENOUGH!
           Devastating Crushing Angry
           Pressure   In my Chest
                            Shoulders

Grandparents   Me   Parents

You have added yourself, have you forgiven yourself? Time to do this; you have been the enforcer of the belief and the continuous negative thoughts. To forgive you and ask for forgiveness, can be very difficult and could take some time. Let's start with writing down I forgive me.

_____

_____

_____

Notes

As you wrote I forgive me how are you feeling? What are your thoughts?

_____

_____

_____

Now let's say a prayer for you. Here is a suggestion to start with:

Dear God, thank you for today, tomorrow, and yesterday. Thank you for filling me with your love as I walk through the process of changing my thoughts. As I look at where my thoughts may have come from, I ask you to stand with me as I forgive me, and I ask for your forgiveness as well. My intention was not to contribute to the negative thoughts and emotions. I forgive me and according to your word you forgive me. I thank you for walking with me as I find peace, love, and forgiveness. In Jesus name Amen.

Here is space to write your own prayer:

_____

_____

_____

Notes

Chapter Five

Connecting History with Emotions

Now that you have everyone on the list, it's time to take inventory of your thoughts and emotions again.

_____

_____

_____

You can add these thoughts and feelings on the paper

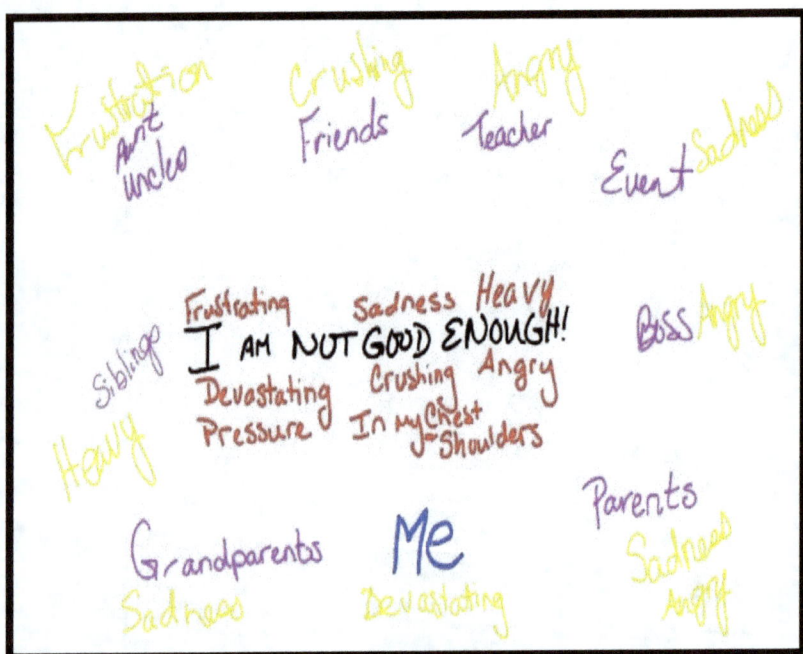

Frustration
Aunt
uncles

Crushing
Friends

Angry
Teacher

Event Sadness

Frustrating   Sadness Heavy
Siblings   I AM NOT GOOD ENOUGH!
Heavy   Devastating Crushing Angry
Pressure   In my Chest
             Shoulders

Boss Angry

Grandparents
Sadness

Me
Devastating

Parents
Sadness
Angry

Notes

As you look at this picture you can start to see how things are connected. When you see your aunt or uncle you may get frustrated, which will lead you to feel like you are not good enough. This could be conscious or unconscious. You could feel this way without even understanding the emotions.

It's time to take inventory again, how are you feeling and what are your thoughts?

_____

_____

_____

This can be hard to do. Make sure you take the time to understand your thoughts and emotions. Process the emotions as they come. Allow the emotions to be there and understand why the emotions are there.

Notes

47

Did you know where the thoughts came from?

_____

_____

_____

Were you aware of how they impacted you?

_____

_____

_____

Which feelings did you feel for each person?

_____

_____

_____

This can be a very hard section. It is hard to see and remember who said what and how you felt. It can also be overwhelming to see that you have taken all these words and emotions that didn't come from God and you became the enforcer of these beliefs about yourself. You took the words from humans and believed them so much that your head has put them on repeat. This can be very hard to digest.

God gives us the free will to do and say what we wish. That means we can believe humans. It's our choice. Now that we have chosen to create new thoughts it's time to create it according to Gods word.

Notes

Chapter Six

God's Word

Now that we know where the thought "I am not good enough!" came from its time to find scripture to disprove this statement.

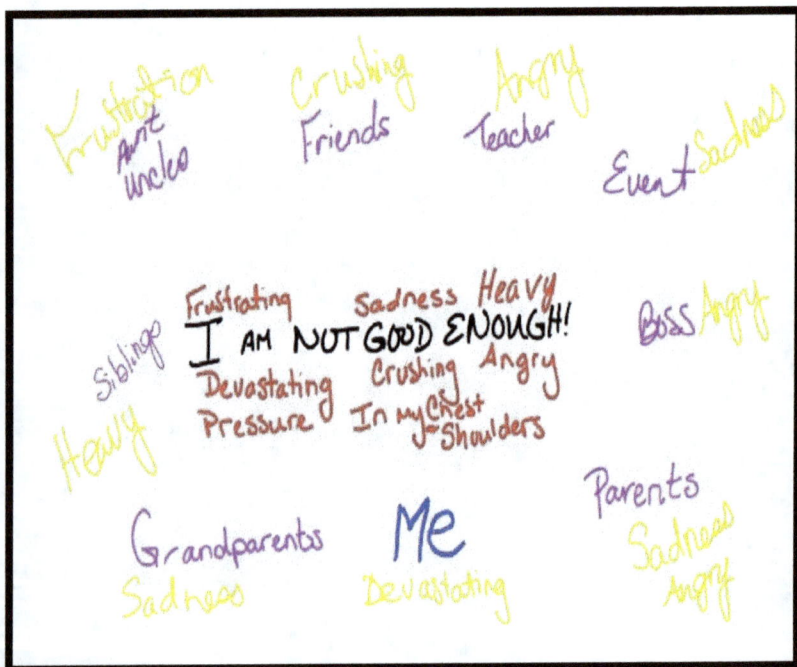

Notes

51

Here are some scriptures for "I am good enough":

"I can do all this through Him who gives me strength." (Philippians 4:13, NIV)

"He has made everything Beautiful in its time." (Ecclesiastes 3:11, NIV)

"My grace is sufficient for you, for my power is made perfect in weakness." (2 Corinthians 12:9, NIV)

"Whatever you do, work at it with all your heart, as working for the lord, not for human masters." (Colossians 3:23, NIV)

Add the scripture you found here:

_____

_____

_____

After seeing the scripture that shows you are good enough, take inventory about how you feel and what additional thoughts might be going through your head.

_____

_____

_____

We have found scripture that has proven our thoughts to be false. Is it time to make a choice to either believe the false thoughts in your head or create new thoughts and start to live in the path that God has for you.

Notes

Chapter Seven

Diving into God's Purpose

Let's compare the scripture and the words that people have said. What scripture that you found canceled out the feelings and thoughts surrounding each person?

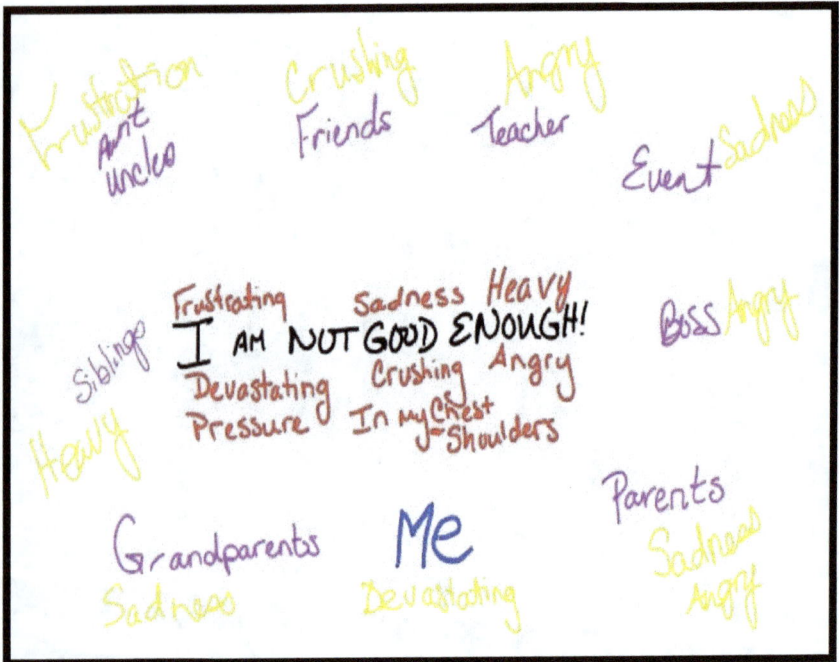

Notes

Let's start with boss and the emotion is angry. Out of the scripture we found which one feels like it cancels out the thoughts and emotions surrounding your boss? Or maybe you feel a different scripture will do a better job of canceling those thoughts and emotions. For our example I am going to use: "whatever you do, work at it with all your heart, as working for the lord, not for human masters," (Colossians 3:23, NIV) to cancel the emotion of anger towards the boss. Now let's add this scripture over boss/anger.

Notes

57

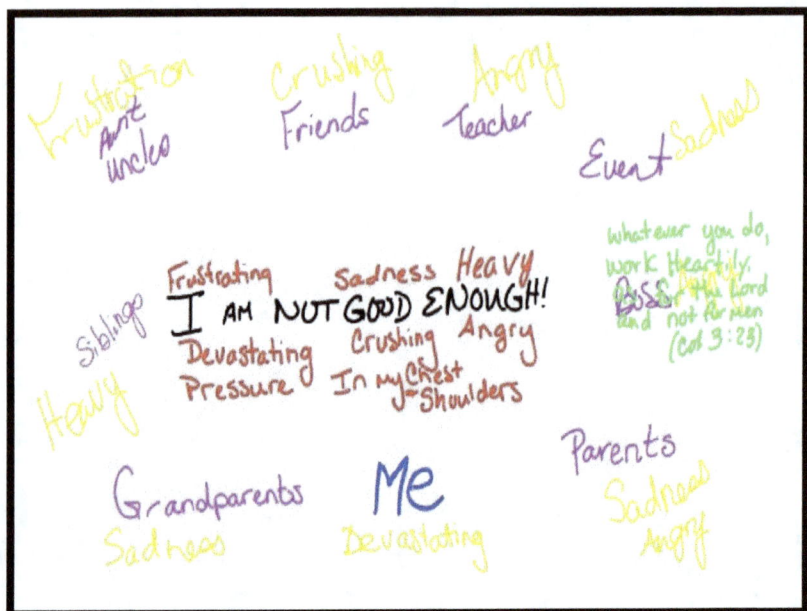

Frustration
aunt
uncle
Crushing
Friends
Angry
Teacher
Event Sadness

Siblings
Frustrating   Sadness Heavy
I AM NOT GOOD ENOUGH!
Devastating Crushing Angry
Pressure In my Chest
Shoulders

Heavy

whatever you do,
work Heartily,
as for the Lord
and not for men
(Col 3:23)

Grandparents
Sadness

Me
Devastating

Parents
Sadness
Angry

Now do the same for every person and event you have on your paper. As we go through the list, we can find scripture to cancel out the negative thoughts and emotions. This process may take some time. You can add as much scripture as you feel is needed.

The scripture that has been added to the paper are to support the statement "I am good enough" and counters the negative thoughts and/or emotions. Some of the scriptures are placed over thoughts or people others are placed in the white of the paper. This can be done in many ways and can take time to find the scripture that proves the negative thoughts and/or emotions false.

Notes

Called according to His Purpose (Romans 8:28)

You have Been Set apart for His... (Deut 14:2)

Fear not...

Friends

In all your Ways acKnowledge Him and He will make Straight your path (Prov 26)

And the Peace of God which Surpasses... (Phil 4:7)

Trust in the Lord...

Show me your ways, Lord, teach me your... (Psalm 25:4)

Whatever you do, work... for the Lord and not for men (Col 3:23)

Frustrating   Sadness Heavy
I AM NOT GOOD ENOUGH!
Devastating   Crushing   Angry
Pressure   In my Chest   Shoulders
(Phil. 4:13)

Me

Grandparents

Parents

You are the light of the world (Matthew 5:14)

(1 Cor. 13:7)

(Romans 15:7)

As we look at all the scripture that makes the negative core thought false, we may ask ourselves many questions such as, "Why have I chosen humans to believe and not God?" and/or "How do I let go of human expectation?" and /or "Now what do I do with this information?" These are all good questions so let's explore some possibilities.

Why do we choose the things humans say over Gods word? This can look different for everyone but here is a possibility. We can see and touch humans, they are easier to believe and follow. As children we start life with humans teaching us, it is natural to follow them. As we develop a relationship with God, we start to believe the love and grace He has for each person. Our relationship is a choice because God has given us free will. You just need to declare that Jesus is your Savior.

Notes

61

How do I let go of human expectations? I believe the Bible answers this with a question. "Am I now trying to win the approval of human beings, or of God?" (Galatians 1:10, NIV). When you have an expectation you feel you need to meet, ask yourself is this God, am I trying to win Gods approval? Then take inventory of your thoughts and emotions. Are they directed toward the Goodness of God or the approval of human beings?

Now what do I do with this information? As we look at our paper, we see that scripture has overtaken the paper. We need to start to correct the thoughts that don't live up with the scripture we have chosen. When you have a negative thought such as "I am not good enough" you say to yourself that is not true according to the word because the word says (read your paper).

Notes

As you take those negative thoughts captive and start to create new thoughts according to the Bible the negative starts to fade away. Until one day all you can see is God's word.

Notes

As you can see on this paper, we now only have the words that are supporting "I am Enough".

> Called according to His Purpose (Romans 8:28)
>
> And the Peace of God which surpasses all understanding will Guard your heart and mind (Phil 4:7)
>
> In all your ways acknowledge Him, and He will Make Straight your Path (Prov 3:6)
>
> Fear not, for I am with you (Isaiah 41:10)
>
> You have Been set apart and Chosen for His Purpose (Deut 14:2)
>
> Show me your ways, Lord; teach me your Paths (Psalm 25:4)
>
> Trust in the Lord with all your heart (Prov 3:5)
>
> I am Enough (Phil. 4:13)
>
> I can do all this through Him who gives me Strength
>
> Whatever you do, work Heartily, as for the Lord and not for men (Col. 3:23)
>
> You are the light of the world (Matthew 5:14)
>
> You have filled My Heart with greater Joy (Psalm 4:7)
>
> Love Never Gives up (1 Cor. 13:7)
>
> Accept on another, then, just as Christ accepted you, in order to bring Praise to God (Romans 15:7)

Notes

Chapter Eight

I Am Enough

Now that we have found we are enough according to the Bible, how do we maintain our new belief? We start by reading the Bible verses at least three times a day to create a new way of thinking. As we say all the verses, we keep taking inventory on our thoughts and feelings. We acknowledge the change in ourselves including our thoughts and emotions.

This change is not easy and can take some time. Just remember the old negative thoughts came from many years ago and from many sources, this new positive thought is just you, God and God's word. It takes time and work to stop the old and create the new.

The Bible has shown us that the saying is false along with the lies from the humans that we believed. The Bible has said that we in fact are good enough. The sentence that we have believed for all our lives we have proven to be false according to the Bible. We now have to turn the page over and rewrite it as "I am good enough".

This new understanding of this thought is a way that we can not only take each thought captive but can start to change our thoughts to match what the Bible says about us. Changing these will help us love ourselves and start to find a better understanding of what God has for us.

Notes

God loves us and it is time for us to believe and have faith in that rather than in humans. Now that you have done this activity you have proven that you are good enough. As you choose what God has to say not what humans have to say, you can now change the statement to; "I am Good enough for God." You know this because you have proven it with God's word.

This is not simple you will need to do this over and over and over again until you find the positives in every day. God wants us to be who He created not who the humans influenced to be negative. Let's celebrate the truth and hold the negative thoughts captive and adjust them to meet and hold true to Gods word.

Notes

Notes

Notes

Notes

9 781960 046000